Kyrie Irving

An inspiring biography of one of basketball's greatest players!

Table of Contents

Introduction

Thank you for taking the time to pick up this book about Kyrie Irving!

This book aims to serve as a biography of the legendary NBA player, Kyrie Irving, and his career so far.
In the following chapters, we will dive into the life and career of Kyrie. You will learn about his childhood, his high school and college experiences, his time in the NBA, and what might be next for the NBA champion!

Hopefully you can draw inspiration from the many stories of Irving's dedication, persistence, and humility shared throughout this book. Kyrie Irving has already achieved a lot in his short career, but there is definitely a lot more to come!

Once again, thanks for choosing this book, I hope you enjoy it!

Chapter 1: Who is Kyrie Irving?

They say that a boy's first hero is their Dad. Kyrie Irving has proved this to be true, after following in his father's footsteps. Kyrie's Dad, Drederick Irving, was also a professional basketball player. He was a college baller for Boston University. He later on played for the Bulleen Boomers in Melbourne, Australia. As a young boy, Irving was fond of watching his Dad's professional games.

Taking inspiration from his father, Irving was an active student-athlete in high school. He spent his prime high school years in Montclair Kimberley Academy. Later on, he transferred to St. Patrick High School, where he played together with Michael Kidd-Gilchrist. He became a brilliant and promising player at both schools. His record in Montclair Kimberly Academy is a whopping average of 26.5 points, 10.3 assists, 3.6 steals, and 4.8 rebounds.

As a teenage basketball superstar, he also played for the Road Runners of the Amateur Athletic Union.

He later on studied at Duke University for a brief period of time. He started playing for the Duke University in 2009 with his head coach, Mike Krzyzewski. Krzyzewski has constantly trained and guided him.

Kyrie was a consistent key player throughout the first eight games of the season, with an average of 17.4 points, from an impressive 52.3 percent shooting. His college basketball record also includes a per-game average of 3.8 rebounds, 5.1 assists, and 1.5 steals.

His impressive performance at college and great potential helped him land the first overall pick in the 2011 NBA draft.

Irving's basketball journey wasn't easy, but he is proof that hard work reaps abundant rewards. Alongside his sky-high achievements is an inspiring story of not giving up on his dreams.

For several seasons, he played side-by-side with LeBron James and Kevin Love, which made the Cleveland Cavaliers a towering contender. They were known as the Cavaliers "Big Three". As the Big Three, they worked together to make their team one of the East Conference's strongest lineups.

Most people, at the age of 22, have just gotten out of college and are still looking for opportunities in the professional world. There are others who, at that age, are still confused about what path they are going to take. But Kyrie Irving is a gifted exception. At the age of 22, Kyrie was already a two-time NBA All-Star and a Rookie of the Year awardee. In a short span of two years, an NBA All-Star MVP Award had already landed into his skilled hands.

In 2016, Irving played for the United States in the Summer Olympics where they won the gold model. This elevated him to elite ranks, making him just the fourth player to win both an NBA championship and an Olympic Gold Medal in the same year. The other three players holding that record are LeBron James, Michael Jordan, and Scottie Pippen.

He was also one of the United States' representatives in the 2014 FIBA Basketball Cup. He was a starter in all nine games they played in the tournament. He played well throughout the tournament, including a 26-point performance in the gold-medal game.

Kyrie Irving's most impressive skill on the court would be his ball-handling ability. This is an area in which he separates himself from the other point guards. Sharing some tips on achieving this kind of ability, he says that practice is the key. He says that anyone may begin with even the most basic steps first, like crossovers behind the back and between the legs. Then, let these simple steps work in combination. His key to being excellent on the court is simply preparedness.

But there's more to Irving than his dribbling skills. He is also a great thinker. He makes sure that his every move is calculated. He sees action on the court as a meditation, and looks at the game as a statistician; saying that a lot can happen in just a split second.

This makes Irving more than just a hardcourt player. He is an influencer. He often reminds everyone that he wants to be remembered as someone who excelled beyond the hardcourt. In fact, he also ventured into social media advertisings when he teamed up with Pepsi. Irving's Pepsi campaign has garnered millions of views and people began calling him as Uncle Drew, the character he portrayed in that social experiment.

With its success, the producers decided to create a movie based on that campaign, with Kyrie Irving taking the lead role.

He is a champion to his friends not just because he's a basketball superstar, but because of who he is as a person. According to peers, Irving is the kind of man who just wants to have fun. Old classmates and colleagues attest to Kyrie as being down-to-earth, and an easy company. A lot of people swear that Kyrie is an outgoing person and he has remained humble despite all his achievements.

Alongside players like Stephen Curry, Isaiah Tomas, Daniel Millard, and Derick Rose; Kyrie Irving showcases the essence of being a low-key, humble basketball player.

A 19-year-old, Irving was able to establish himself as a promising newbie right after the Draft. His impressive and consistent performances gave him a good start in the NBA. He had an average of 18 and a half points and nearly six assists in every game in his first season.

Unfortunately, despite Irving's contribution to the team, the Cavaliers took a long time to build up their wins. This led some to doubt the young guard's ability as a leader and as a player. People began comparing him to other point guards who were unable to lead their teams to a championship, like Derick Rose, John Wall, Chris Paul, and Kyle Lowry. But, Kyrie was still very young, and his performance on the court was enough to attract LeBron James.

When Kevin Love and LeBron James arrived, the people of Cleveland were more hopeful in their basketball team than ever. With the three key players working side-by-side, the Cleveland Cavaliers had entered a new and hopeful era.

Unfortunately, the Cavaliers faced a lot of pressure due to expectations of an instant win. Fans and the entire basketball world were demanding quick results. It was going to take time for the new team to learn to play together.

For a young player, Irving handled this scrutiny incredibly well. He was able to put his head down, work hard, and learn from the experience and guidance of LeBron James. Together, they ultimately found success – but we'll get into that later!

Chapter 2: Kyrie's Childhood

On the 23rd of March, 1992, a future basketball superstar was born in Melbourne Australia. He was named Kyrie Andrew Irving.

His older sister, Asia, was also born in Melbourne. However, their family moved soon after to Orange, New Jersey, USA where Kyrie spent his childhood.

Kyrie's passion for basketball was influenced by his father. His Dad was also a professional basketball player whose career was quite extended. Kyrie says that his father's love for basketball was very contagious. Basketball was a huge part of Kyrie's childhood, and was a daily routine since his infancy.

His father, Drederick, would often bring Kyrie to his games. As early as his elementary days, Kyrie received invitations to be part of his peer's basketball teams.

It was in fourth grade when he first began dreaming about playing in the NBA.

After a school trip where he was allowed to play at the Continental Airlines Arena, Kyrie promised to himself that he was going to the NBA. He wrote that dream on a small piece of paper.

His father, being Kyrie's first mentor, felt that this dream was firmly planted in Kyrie's heart. However, he also knew that his son was going to face a lot of challenges on his way to achieving that dream. His own experiences had taught him that a goal as towering as playing in the NBA would be difficult.

Despite the challenges ahead, Drederick also knew from the beginning that Kyrie was going to have a promising future because of his determination. He saw nothing but an unbelievably serious commitment from his young son. He saw that Kyrie spent long hours pushing himself in training. With this, Drederick felt that he needed to help his son in planning for his future. The decision to plan ahead was influenced by

Drederick's own experiences in the field of basketball. He wanted to extend every bit of help and guidance he could to prepare Kyrie for achieving his NBA dreams.

Just like any other basketball player, Drederick also dreamt of playing in the NBA, but he admits that his own mistakes and shortcomings prevented him from entering the prestigious league. He didn't want Kyrie to be stopped by the same mistakes.

Kyrie's mother, Elizabeth, passed away when he was still very young. Her passing made it hard for Kyrie and his family. However, this tragedy did make Kyrie and his father even closer.

The physical basketball training had its fair share of challenges. At first, Kyrie wasn't very aggressive on the court. He was almost a timid player. He appeared to lack confidence, despite all of the belief that his father had in him.

Drederick wanted to make sure that their trainings would result in an over-all development of not just Kyrie's basketball skills, but more importantly his character. Their weekend trainings included drills like dribbling multiple balls at various speeds, handling balls wrapped in plastic, and dribbling tennis balls.

These training sessions sculpted Kyrie's prolific ball-handling ability. As both a mentor and a father, Drederick made sure that Kyrie's competitive spirit would not break his humility. He constantly reminded Kyrie that while he is asleep, someone else was training hard to be better than him, so he had better work double when he wakes up.

With continuous and diligent practice, Drederick was able to help improve Kyrie's game. Seeing his son's improvements, he had the confidence to enroll Kyrie into the New Jersey's Amateur Athletic Union Roadrunners Basketball Program.

Chapter 3: Kyrie's High School Career

Kyrie had his first taste of a more serious basketball career when he played for the Montclair Kimberley Academy. He averaged sixteen points per game in his freshman year. Because of his consistent and impressive performances, he received the Freshman of the Year Award. However, despite the good basketball records, he was still considered a late bloomer as compared to other high school basketball standouts in the past.

In his sophomore year, Irving improved a lot through the help of his trainer Sandy Pyonin. His scoring improved to 26-points per game, which helped him lead Montclair University to its very first New Jersey Prep B State title.

Kyrie even had an impressive 47-point performance that season. According to him teammates, Kyrie always seemed to rise to the occasion.

Despite his growing achievements and praise received, people could always see Irving's humility both on and off the court. Tony Jones, Kyrie's coach at Montclair, had nothing but praise for his exemplary attitude. Jones said that it's not every day that we get to see extremely good people, like Kyrie, who take every opportunity with a grounded attitude. He added that sometime kids the same age as Kyrie, and with the same achievements as him, would often show off a diva-like attitude. But Kyrie was far from that, and showed off nothing but his humility.

As his skills improved, Kyrie also needed to become more competitive. He later on transferred to St. Patrick School, which is one of New Jersey's more advanced basketball prep schools.

Irving had remarkable growth as player at St. Patrick's. As a junior, he played with an average of 6-assists and 17-points per game. It was also in junior year that he helped St. Patrick's win its third State Championship.

In the tender phase of senior year, he had already established himself as one of the best players not just in his State, but in

America in general. Basketball enthusiasts and media often included Kyrie in their Top 5 or Top 10 high school players.

This opened a lot of doors and opportunities for Kyrie. He received offers from numerous universities and programs. They saw Kyrie's abilities as a big chance for potential championships.

Despite the numerous offers, Irving wanted to choose a program that would take advantage of not just his basketball abilities, but his brains as well. This principle helped him narrow down the choices to Texas A&M University, Seaton Hall University, Georgia Tech, Duke University, and Western Kentucky.

Choosing a university was a crucial decision for Irving because it is no secret that college programs are a good stepping stone to a professional basketball career. On October 22, 2009, he announced that he had chosen Duke University.

Irving says that he was impressed with Duke University's teamwork. He saw that everyone, from top to bottom, had something to contribute to the team. Duke University also seemed to have a deep understanding of basketball. These were the extra factors that Kyrie was looking for. He says that it was Duke's brotherhood, trust, and love that pushed him into choosing the team.

Before he finally started at Duke, he still had a year left in his high school basketball career. After selecting Duke, he seemed to step up his performance on the court even more.

His continuous growth as a player was evident when he led the St. Patrick's to 24-3 record in his senior year. Irving contributed 27.4-points per game on average, and led the team to finish in first place at the Union Country Tournament. Unfortunately, St. Patrick's was not allowed to participate in the State Tournament due to breaking the rules on off-season practice. Nevertheless, Kyrie still had a promising future ahead of him.

Because he was a top college recruit, he had the opportunity to play in the McDonald's All-American and the Jordan Brand Classic where he became a co-MVP. These games were quite huge, as they let Kyrie test himself against the country's best

players his age. All of this was just preparing him for a short, but
impressive, college career.

Chapter 4: The Making of a Superstar

Sandy Pyonin was Kyrie's trainer during his formative years. Irving seemed to be fortunate in being surrounded by the right people when he was younger. Pyonin was the best trainer Kyrie could possibly want. He was very diligent and dedicated to helping him. Their sessions included full-skills development trainings, as well as a focus on nurturing work ethic.

He was Irving's constant teacher during his high school years. They would eagerly train during summer; resting only one day per week.

After the persistent physical skills training, Pyonin would train Kyrie through one of his most extreme conditioning drills. He would get Kyrie to play a full court on-one-one game; aiming for a score of nothing less than 100, but counting every shot as only one point. They would play this drill with no breaks.

Other alumni trained by Pyonin say that he was the kind of coach who not only focused on the physical skills, but also on character development, decision-making abilities, and court awareness. Pyonin was very much willing to help his trainees straighten their vision towards a goal. He didn't want his trainees lurking in the streets. One of his alumni, Randy Foye, said in an interview that Pyonin helped him to become more than just a failed statistic.

Pyonin is a true expert in the field of basketball. He is a basketball connoisseur and a tough trainer. His credentials include being an all-around coach-teacher at the Golda Och Academy. He has coached boys' teams for middle school soccer, middle school basketball, and varsity basketball. He has also coached girls' varsity softball team at the Golda Och.

He was also the coach of the New Jersey Road Runners AAU Team for thirty years. Under his supervision, the team has won 70 states and 3 national championships. But overall, the AAU has garnered 2,306 wins under his leadership. Throughout his time as an AAU coach, he was able to send more than 300 players to the Division 1 level. His tough training mentality has helped to produce more than 30 professional basketball players; many of whom landed in the NBA in early rounds of the draft.

Touching the lives of many successful basketball players has made him a renowned basketball guru. More than being a legendary coach, others also brand him as an NBA Dreammaker. They compare Pyonin to a human machine that produces high-quality NBA players.

Pyonin was an important spark in Kyrie's life. He was the spark that ignited and brought more fire to Kyrie's work ethic, vision, and Drederick's life lessons. He ignited the fire that polished Kyrie into a fine player for the Duke University.

Pyonin and Irving's relationship began when Drederick first found out about the New Jersey coach. He heard a lot of good things about the coach, and so he asked him to coach his son.

Irving and Pyonin trained six days a week during summer, and each session lasted for five to ten hours. The extreme trainings also aimed to condition Kyrie's mental abilities. While most coaches fail to emphasize the mental aspect of basketball, Pyonin was a firm believer that mental conditioning was essential in order to succeed.

When the humbled and grateful Irving received his NBA Rookie of the Year Award in 2012, he did not forget to look back on the person who molded him into the professional player that he had become. In his speech, he mentioned the name of his high school coach, Sandy Pyonin, and acknowledged him for being a big part of his success.

Chapter 5: Irving's College Career

Kyrie Irving was a promising addition to the Duke University Basketball team when he jumped on board with the Plumlee Brothers and other veterans in the 2010-2011 Season. Everyone was optimistic that another NCAA National championship title was heading Duke's way.

The previous year was also a sweet one for the Blue Devils as they bagged the school's fourth national title. With Irving finally joining their roster of players, Duke was in high hopes for a repeat championship.

Irving's strength did not disappoint his coach, Mike Krzyewski's expectations. He was able to lead the team to a good start. He led the team to a 10-1 record for the eleven games he played for Duke. Irving left with an outstanding record of 17.6-points per game, and a field goal percentage of 53 percent. He also recorded an impressive 46 percent shooting from 3. Meanwhile, his shooting percentage at the charity stripe or free throw line was an efficient and remarkable 90 percent.

In a game against Michigan State, on December 1st, Irving dropped 31-points on an impressive 66 percent shooting. He made history on that day by being the fourth freshman to score 30 or more points for Duke. He also held the Number 1 record for having the most free throws made by a freshman, with a total of 13.

In a first-of-the-season game against Harvard University, he wowed the fans with 9-assists. This was the highest number of assists ever by a freshman during a season opener.

Despite the historical and extremely efficient performances, unfortunate events would shorten Irving's college career. A toe injury would abruptly end his career after 11 games, and darken his supposed bright future at Duke.

Irving, and everyone around him, had to take precautions and focus on his health. Although he did not break any bones, the

injury was still quite serious, with moderate ligament damage
suffered.

Irving, a strong favorite for the National Freshman of the Year,
was injured in a game against Bradley in December 2010. He
got the injury on a drive to the basket. He stumbled on his way
to the bench and his facial expression was a clear indication of a
serious injury.

Medical examinations and healing took months. The Irving
family had personal talks discussing plans for Kyrie's career.
After considering the options, on April 6 2011, an
announcement was made. It was announced that Kyrie would
leave college early to enter the NBA Draft.

Irving felt that it was just the right decision to make. Colleagues,
friends and family completely supported him in this decision.
He made one promise to his Dad, though. He promised him that
he would finish his degree despite joining the NBA.

Chapter 6: The Start of Irving's NBA Dreams

Many basketball enthusiasts were not impressed with the NBA's 2011 Draft. At that time, people made remarks that it might just be the poorest and weakest class in history.

Irving was strongly craved by every franchise. Many teams were desperate for talent at the point guard position. Every franchise knew that Irving's rare abilities and well-polished plays could be an advantage to them.

On May 17, 2011, the most awaited NBA draft lottery pick happened. Audiences and other attendees at the Prudential Center, New Jersey were looking forward to the upcoming results. Based on statistics, the Minnesota Timberwolves were favored to get the number 1 pick. The team had a poor performance the previous season, and they left a miserable record of 17-65. But historically, the team has always had a difficult time with luck. They've never been won the first pick in a draft.

Next on the list were the Cavaliers and the Raptors. These two teams were also having their fair share of challenges as they lost their franchise players to the Miami Heat. The Cavaliers lost LeBron James, and the Raptors lost Chris Bosh.

The preceding draft years were not bad for both the Cavaliers and the Raptors. In 2003, the Cavaliers seemed to have been touched by luck when they won LeBron James in the draft. While in 2007, despite the very slim probability of an 8.8 percent chance of winning, the Raptors miraculously won the lottery.

While still in their post-LeBron rebuilding process, the lottery would favor the Cleveland Cavaliers. They regained their hope as they won the lottery, and the No.1 selection for the next month's draft.

The Minnesota Timberwolves, on the other hand, won the No. 2 pick.

To preserve and even raise his value, Kyrie trained with numerous coaches, including Robin Pound. Pound is an NBA veteran known for his strength and conditioning workouts. In his speech in front of the Cleveland media after receiving the Rookie of the Year Award, Irving thanked Pound for being the best trainer out there.

Pound, on the other hand, has noted Irving's strong sense of competitiveness. Irving seemed like waking up every morning ready to impress everyone. This kind of characteristic is crucial in every aspiring NBA Player. Pound, being a veteran trainer for the NBA, had already seen a lot of players come and go. After years of working with NBA players, Pound has mastered the ability of measuring a rookie's possible longevity in the NBA. His main criteria for this is none other than competitiveness – the exact thing that he has seen in Irving throughout their training sessions.

Having a great trainer to help him, Irving was also able to make the most of his draft workouts. He was clear in saying that being the Number 1 pick was not his priority. He just wanted to focus mainly on the pre-draft private workouts; no matter what team would choose him. In fact, he decided to forgo every distraction, like deactivating his twitter account.

After the draft workouts, every sign was suggesting that Irving would be picked by the Cavaliers. He was, after all, every franchise's top choice. Through his topnotch skills, he had successfully set himself apart from the others. He was the consensus top pick.

Comparisons between him and LeBron James even began to surface. LeBron was also Cleveland's first draft pick in 2003.

Drederick, Kyrie's father, was nothing but proud and happy for his son. However, he was open in saying that his son is a different player from LeBron James. He assured everyone that Kyrie would bring his own style of play to the table. Drederick also added that he just wanted Kyrie to be himself; just the best version of what he could be, and not a copy of anyone else.

June 23, 2011 was a special day for Kyrie Irving. It was the 2011 NBA Draft. Experts' and basketball enthusiasts' prediction came true – Kyrie Irving became the Cleveland Cavalier's top pick in the NBA Draft.

What made the night more magical was that the draft took place in New Jersey – Kyrie's hometown. The dream that a fourth-grader wrote on a piece of paper was finally fulfilled.

Irving said that the evening of June 23, 2011 will always be a memorable moment for him. Irving was grateful and confident that he was worth the pick. He assured everyone that the rehabilitation process for his injury was successful. In fact, he looked very comfortable as he walked up the stairs to shake hands with David Stern. There were signs of happiness, but none of an injury. His health was okay and he believed he could be instrumental in rebuilding the Cavaliers after LeBron's departure.

Despite the overwhelming feelings of gratefulness and excitement, Irving knew that being drafted was just the first step in a tough journey ahead. He firmly held onto the mantra that his father had instilled in his young mind – "Stay hungry and humble".

It is no secret that some players just come and go. When fame and money begin creeping into some players' minds, they get distracted and lose sight of the goal. Irving just refused to let that happen.

Just like in any NBA draft, as the number 1 pick, Irving was doubted by some. There were those who maliciously speculated whether Irving was worth it. The doubts and questions surrounding Irving stemmed from his short stint at Duke University. People were quick to point out that the 6-foot-4 top pick had only one season at Duke, where he only played eleven games.

But owners of the Cleveland Cavaliers said that the potential they saw in Irving was enough to outweigh his lack of college experience. This belief in Kyrie certainly paid off.

Chapter 7: Irving's Rookie Year

In 2011, the NBA had its fourth lockout season in history. This meant Irving had to wait for half a year before he began his Rookie Season.

There was a labor disagreement between the NBA owners and the players. The players wanted the NBA to be something similar to Major League Basketball. Their side wanted guaranteed salaries whether the player performed well or not.

On the other hand, the NBA owners wanted it the other way around. They wanted more revenue sharing, and smaller salaries. They also wanted the power to let go of a player who doesn't perform well.

In a nutshell, the dispute was about designing a system that would benefit both the owners and the players.

Others looked at the Armageddon season as an opportunity to unwind. But Irving saw it as a time to reflect on his goals and prepare hard for the upcoming games. He continued training to keep him physically and mentally sharp. He took the lockout as an opportunity to prove that he was the most game-faced and ready out of all the 2011 rookies.

On the morning of November 26, 2011, the NBA owners and players reached a tentative resolution that ended the lockout. The NBA was back in business and Irving had long been ready for it.

One of Irving's advantageous abilities, is that he knows how to choose his battles. He knows which circumstances will be good or bad for him. He knows that comparison to anyone else will not help him reach the goal of becoming the best version of himself. He just wants to play like Irving and not anyone else. And this mindset has helped him maintain his humility and grounded attitude, and not be distracted by the LeBron comparisons.

Unfortunately, the spotlight did not help Kyrie in his first real NBA game. The media attention and pressure brought him jitters. His first night as a professional player on the NBA court was an eye-opener for him. He realized that the opportunity to be in the NBA was a huge and tough one.

On his debut as a professional player, the Cavaliers lost to the Toronto Raptors with a score of 104-96. The opening game for the Cavaliers was a long night for the 19-year-old point guard. It was his first NBA heartbreak, too.

Still, Irving managed to score 6 points. He also had 7 assists and 1 turnover. It was a decent game for a first-timer.

He used this loss as a fire to ignite his determination even more. He was able to rebuild himself from the jitters of his debut. Despite the public pressure, Irving's attitude and work ethic remained strong.

In January, he was able to get more comfortable and learn more about the NBA style of play. He drastically improved his performance; shutting the doubters down. In fact, Irving began having a phenomenal Rookie Season. He emerged as a dominant first-year player.

Irving's statistics improved into double figures as he marked a career-high record of 32-points against the New Jersey Nets. He has successfully led the team to a record of 8-12 at the end of January. His consistent numbers helped him be the recipient of the Eastern Conference's Rookie of the Month Award.

The Rookie of the Month Award didn't end in January. In fact, Irving bagged the award for the first three months of 2012; making him a grand slam awardee.

The Rookie of the Month Award is given to the NBA newbie who consistently has good performances. Irving was consistently ranked first in scoring, free throw percentage, and three-point percentage among all Eastern Conference rookies.

In February, Irving had the most 20-point games by a rookie in that month. He had also averaged 6.8 points per quarter. He marked a record of 31 consecutive free throws. His .953 free throw percentage set a historical record of being the highest monthly free throw percentage by a rookie since 1998.

In a game against Sacramento in February, Irving dropped 23-points in 39 minutes. At the last quarter, with only 2.9 seconds left on the clock, the Cavaliers were behind by one. Kyrie managed to score a buzzer beater to win the game.

A few days later, Irving set a career-high record of 11 assists and only 2 turnovers in a game against the Hornets.

Thanks to his impressive performances, Irving was invited to the NBA All-Star Weekend. He was invited to participate in the Skills Challenge where he competed with elite ballers like Russell Westbrook, Deron Williams, John Wall, Tony Parker, and 2011 MVP Stephen Curry. The competition was not a serious game but rather just a cool and fun activity. However, for a rookie to be invited to such event and compete against senior players is a big thing.

Irving was also asked to play in the Rising Stars Challenge where he dominated other players. He showcased his fast-paced playing skills as well as his open-court and aerial skills in a game between two teams selected by NBA legends Shaquille O'Neal and Charles Barkley. Irving was picked to join the latter's team.

Irving impressed with a massive 34 points and a perfect 8 for 8 from beyond the arc. Within just 27 minutes of play, he managed to record nine assists, two steals, and only three turnovers. Critiques remarked that Irving had the ability to make the other newbies appear like they didn't have even half of his basketball prowess. He outshined all his contemporaries including Wizards' John Wall and Pistons' Brandon Knight.

Irving went home with an MVP Award for the Rising Stars Challenge. More importantly, he gained a lot more respect and admiration that day. The All-Star Weekend was an opportunity for Irving to prove everyone just how talented and grounded he is.

March was also a good month for Irving as he received his third consecutive Rookie of the Month Award. He was the leading rookie in terms of scoring and assists; and second in free throw percentage. On March 9, he set another career-high record of 12 assists in a game against the Oklahoma City Thunder.

In another record-setting game against the Celtics, Irving smoothly made his way to the basket, cut between two defenders and maneuvered a left-handed lay-up that brought his team to victory.

Indeed, Irving was one of the NBA's most sensational rookies in history. To cap off the year, Irving was named the Rookie of the Year. He garnered 117 out of 120 possible first-place votes from a panel consisting of media broadcasters and writers.

 The award was quite unsurprising given the grand slam Rookie of the Month Awards, consistent leadership abilities, statistical prowess, and his overall up-tempo play. His key playing elements included wise instincts in the fourth quarter, nasty crossover dribbles, and an unstoppable desire to score. In fact, Irving was already part of bleacherreport.com's Top 25 sensational rookies even before he was through with his rookie year.

His father, Drederick, was the first person that Kyrie thanked in his Rookie of the Year speech.

When asked to pose for photographers during the Rising Stars awards, Irving lowered down his trophy to make his uniform more visible. He told photographers to make sure that the imprinted "Cleveland" on his jersey was visible in every photograph.

Cavaliers' owner, Dan Gilbert, had nothing but praise for Irving's skill and character. He said that Irving is a fantastic kid with a great heart. He added that Irving has clear passion for basketball and a love for people.

Irving's first year as a professional player was a victorious one. But more importantly, Season 11-12 was a learning experience for him. Irving learned the ropes of the NBA through the help of Cavalier's head coach, Byron Scott.

After Irving's challenging first NBA game, Scott said that public pressure could really affect a rookie's play as he also experienced the same thing. But he believed Irving would improve. Forty-nine more games after that first one, Scott was grateful his player exceeded all his expectations.

At the end of the Season 11-12, the Cavaliers showed improvement by finishing in 13th place in the Eastern Conference. They were just four games behind Detroit which was the 10th placed team. Irving had brought hope to the Cavaliers and all their fans once more.

Chapter 8: NBA Career and Achievements

Sophomore Year: Season 2012-2013

People who doubted Irving in his rookie year were all proven wrong.

Draft season came once again, and the Cavaliers won the Number 4 pick. The Cavaliers used the 4th pick to choose Syracuse University's Dion Waiters.

Just after the draft, the media were focused on whether Waiters could create a dynamic duo with Irving. Doubts begin to surface as the Syracuse' sixth man, Dion Waiters, was given the billing of an instant starter. It was quite unusual for a reserve to belong in the Top 5 picks.

However, the Cavaliers took the bold move of choosing Waiters because they learned a lesson when they picked Irving in the previous year. For the Cavaliers, playing time was quite irrelevant. Kyrie had only 11 games in college and was also doubted because of that. However, Kyrie proved his worth and exceeded everyone's expectations. That's what Waiters was also set to do. The team expected him to be a big help to Irving.

Experts on basketball statistics said that Irving needed to score an average of 22-24 per game, with six-eight assists in order to improve the Cavalier's standing. Irving, once again, met those expectations. He averaged nearly 24 points per game, and six assists in his sophomore year.

It was quite unsurprising to those who had paid attention to the promising performances of last season's Rookie of the Year. Before 2012 ended, the Cavaliers were a .500 ball club.

He was still the Cavaliers' go-to man in terms of shooting. The team was set to lead him to success and vice versa. Irving was a natural team player and his teammates also complimented him well.

In April 2013, Irving and his team mates faced two challenging scenarios that overlapped in the Cavalier's timeline. While the Cavaliers were still in the post-James rebuilding process, their head coach was also set to leave.

The Cavaliers' General Manager, Christ Grant, publicly announced that they had released Byron Scott from coaching the team.

The team was reminded of the frustrations and pain they felt when LeBron James left. It was especially difficult to Irving who seemed to be very appreciative of everyone who extended him a helping hand. Irving has always had a personal relationship with all his mentors, including Byron Scott.

Irving had a special relationship with his first NBA coach. Being drafted by Scott, Irving regarded him as his basketball father. Irving consistently gave his coach due praise for helping him learn the ropes of NBA. He always acknowledges Scott's help in molding him to become the player he is today.

But evidently, shaping up the team's franchise player and everything Scott did for the Cavs were not enough for the management.

After Scott was released from the Cavaliers' management, rumors that Irving might also transfer to another team began circulating. Irving's bond with Scott was comparable to that of a real family's. "I feel that a piece of me is missing", Irving said, after Scott left.

Just a few days after Scott was ousted, Mike Brown was officially announced as the Cavaliers' newest head coach. Brown had already been Cleveland's head coach in 2005-2010. According to the Cavs owner Dan Gilbert and general manager Chris Grant, Brown possessed all the criteria they were looking for in a coach. Brown is a hard worker, has a defensive game plan, and is a proven winner. Through these qualities, Brown was expected to compliment Irving's leadership. The two were expected to jive together in working towards Cleveland's goals.

At 20, Irving had his first All-Star East vs West game. Out of the wide selection of point guards, Irving was chosen for the event.

Kyrie managed to score 15-points for his team. He also participated again in the Rising Stars Challenge where he contributed 32-points to Team Shaq.

Finally, he participated in the NBA Three-Point Shootout where we won with a final score of 23-points.

In another game held in the Mecca of Basketball, Madison Square, he set a career-high record of 41 points. Irving wowed the basketball crowd and connoisseurs with his record-setting performance despite the facial injuries he had suffered the night prior to the game. Irving wore a protective face mask that somehow gave him confidence to attack the basket relentlessly.

Kyrie Irving made history by breaking Michael Jordan's record of being the youngest player to score 40 (or more) points in Madison Square Garden. Jordan was 21 years old when he scored 42 points at MSG, while the record-breaker, Irving was only 20 years old when he scored his 41 points in New York.

Irving ended his sophomore year with an average of 22.5 points per game; with 1.5 steals, 5.9 assists, and 3.7 rebounds.

Season 2013-2014

At 21, Irving was clearly becoming one of the league's elite point guards as he had his third NBA All-Star Weekend appearance.

It was a historical and record-setting night for the NBA. The teams registered a record-setting combined score of 318 points. The East team won with a total score of 163 points, the most ever by a single team.

For the West side, Kevin Durant and Blake Griffin's scores totaled the most number of points registered by two team mates. Both players scored 38-points.

Irving registered good numbers for the East that night. He scored a total of 31-points. He scored 24 of those points in the second half, which tied another record. Irving successfully connected on 3 (out of 6) three-pointer shots. The 3 unsuccessful three-pointers were the only shots he missed out of all the 17 that he attempted.

Irving was on fire in the second half of the game where he dished out seven assists. Irving often went hard to the basket and finished strong. He showed off the competitive spirit that he was known for.

A competitive spirit is often lacking in All-Star Games. But Irving is known for always giving his best to every game he plays – whether it is a serious NBA game or something that's just for fun. He told reporters that it was just right to be competitive because the fans deserve a good show.

More importantly, the 21-year-old Irving made history again by being the second youngest All-Star MVP; next to LeBron James.

James was 21 years old and 1 month when he won his first All-Star MVP in 2006. Irving, on the hand, was 21 years old and 10 months. Both of them were Cavaliers when they won that award.

During the awarding ceremonies, James was asked by the media about his thoughts on Irving. "Kyrie has the total package and I've seen that since he was in high school. I am happy and proud of him", James said.

Even Coach Frank Vogel of Indiana Pacers was impressed with Irving's performance. "Irving is one the best in the world and he has definitely showed that tonight", Vogel said.

Being the humble player that he is, Irving said that the award was not solely for him, but for his entire team. More importantly, he was happy that the All-Star MVP trophy was back in Cleveland.

In a game against the Utah Jazz in February, 2014, Irving had a dominating performance that led him to his first career triple-double. He scored a game-high 21-points, grabbed 10 boards and handed out 12 assists in a 99-97 victory.

However, Irving was not able to bring glory to Cleveland with his impressive solo performances. The season 2013-2014 ended shakily for the Cavaliers. Irving's team dived into a 5 losing streak.

Irving, though, ended the season with the following averages: 20.8 points, 6.1 assists, 3.6 rebounds and 1.5 steals.

Season 2014-2015

Irving's fourth season in the NBA is one of his career highlights. It first began with poor team performances, failures, injuries and a lot of other distractions. There were even issues on the team's chemistry. Rumors had it that the team didn't get along really well which resulted to a losing culture. There were also rumors of other members leaving. Distractions were all around for the Cavaliers, and Irving, being their leading point guard, had a lot of work to do.

Despite his growing list of individual accolades, Irving' team was still stuck in a losing culture.

The Cavaliers management resorted to a total transformation of their team. They were afraid to lose Irving who was nearing the end of his contract. Therefore, they did everything they could to create a team of high-potential players. The management was determined to up their chances by transforming the Lottery Team into a Dream Team.

Aided by some good fortune, the Cavs once again won the lottery for draft pick Number 1. This gave them a hundred percent chance to add Andrew Wiggins.

Cleveland General Manager David Griffin traded plenty of his players. He first sent off forward Sergey Karasev and guard Jarrett Jack to the Brooklyn Nets. They were followed by center Tyler Zeller who went to the Boston Celtics as part of a 3-team deal. Players Christian Drejer, Ilkan Karaman, and Edin Bavcic became acquisitions of Cleveland as they got the draft rights for the three. Also as part of the deal, Marcus Thornton was transferred from Brooklyn to Boston.

Just after the last NBA Finals, rumors of LeBron James returning to Cleveland were the talk of the basketball world. There were strong rumors that Cleveland might be welcoming LeBron back with open arms.

In a touching letter published on a sports website, LeBron James publicly announced that he was indeed going back to the Cleveland Cavaliers. This move was one of the most remarkable and exciting events in basketball history. Fans raved about the possibilities of a total turn-around for Cleveland's destiny as James and Irving form a dynamic 1-2 punch.

However, the NBA world didn't know that there was more to come.

There were also rumors that Cleveland was targeting Minnesota Timberwolves' Kevin Love. The All-Star forward kept quiet about it, but openly said that he wanted to work with James if given the chance. Love and James started their brotherhood when they both played in the Olympics for Team USA.

The rumor of Love joining the Cavaliers left fans with just one question: "Are the Cavaliers willing to sacrifice their Number 1 pick, Andrew Wiggins and his potential for the sake of Kevin Love?"

On June 23, the Cavs management answered that question through their actions. They decided to send off Wiggins together with another Number 1 pick, Anthony Bennett, to Minnesota in exchange for Kevin Love.

This revamp brought a lot of hope to the Cavaliers. With Irving, James, and Love making up the team's so-called Big Three; the Cavs were off to a determined and strong season.

In fact, Cleveland's starting five was considered to be one of the strongest starting line-up in the league. It consisted of the Big Three – Irving, James, and Love – together with Dion Waiters and Anderson Varejao. LeBron's good friend, Mike Miller had also become part of the team.

Irving began the season with a 5-year, $90-million-dollar contract extension. With the new roster of players, the Cavaliers recovered from their previous season's losses. They've went on an eight-game winning streak after losing against Toronto on November 22. Irving averaged 19.3 points per game during that winning streak. In a game against New York Knicks on December 4, he contributed 37-points.

But despite Irving's consistent attitude, the Cavaliers still had inconsistent play on the court. They had highs and lows, and unpredictable wins and losses. The year 2014 ended without much promise, and the future of the Cavaliers was still unclear.

When 2015 kicked in, the Cavaliers won against the Charlotte Hornets in a 91-87 victory. Irving scored 23 points, while Love contributed strongly with 27. However, the inconsistent play still continued. They'd win one game, only to lose the next.

In a game against Houston in January, Irving dropped 38 points. However, despite his good individual performance he was not able to lift up the team and they lost with a final score of 93-105. That was their seventh loss in nine games.

Despite the six-game losing streak, Irving and James were still able to bring the team back into contention. The pair led their team on a 12-game winning streak, in which Irving averaged 24.5 points per game. He has set another career-high record of 55-points in a game against Portland.

Irving again made another history when he scored a new career-high 57 points in a game against the San Antonio Spurs. It was the highest number of points scored by a player in a regular-season game against a defending champion.

In that game, Irving was able to shoot a buzzer-beater three-pointer that brought his team into overtime, where they finished with a 128-125 win.

Irving was able to help his team reach the NBA Finals where they battled against the Golden State Warriors. Irving, though, had to leave the finals' first game as he suffered from a knee injury. The injury was identified as a fractured kneecap which resulted in Irving being ruled out for the rest of the series, and leaving him in recovery for 4 months.

The Cavs may have lost the championship to the Warriors, but finishing off as the No. 2 seed in the Eastern Conference was much better than their previous year's performance.

Irving took quite some time to heal his injury. His medical team gave him the go-ahead to play again on December 20. Season 15-16 may not have started well for Irving, but what's important is that it ended in sweet victory.

For the first time in franchise history, and in Irving's fifth season as a professional basketball player, the Championship title landed into the hands of the Cavaliers. The Cavs' Game 7 win against the Warriors was the first time in NBA history that a team has overcome a 3-1 deficit to bring home the Championship Title.

It was no doubt that Irving made big contributions in the Championship win. Actually, it was Kyrie Irving who fired the winning shot that sealed the game at 92-89, and brought the Larry O'Brien Trophy to Cleveland

With only 53 seconds left on the clock, Irving had a crucial battle with Stephen Curry. Irving stepped back on the left wing as his opponent came closer. In what seemed to be the most crucial 53 seconds in Irving's life, he bravely shot the ball as high and true as he could. The ball fell perfectly into the net, and secured them the lead.

Irving contributed a total of 27 points and 11 assists in the team's Game 7 victory.

Chapter 9: A New Home for Irving

At 28, Irving seemed to have already experienced everything that a professional baller encounters in his entire career. He had the lows – being unable to lead his team to victory, being sidelined for months, team revamping, injuries, doubters, and non-believers. But he also had his ups – accolades, off the court projects, a championship, and gaining people's respect.

He survived and did all of these in the comfort of his Cleveland uniform. Cleveland was his home for six years.

Before the year 2017 came to an end, Kyrie Irving was still showing off his basketball wizardry. But that time, in a different uniform.

From the Cleveland Cavaliers, Kyrie Irving moved to the Boston Celtics. Kyrie's trading has been covered with controversy. The Cavs management said that it was Irving who asked for the trade.

Irving, on the other hand, has remained silent about it. He decided not to speak during the process. But as soon as the trade was over, Kyrie had some clarifications to make.

According to Irving, it's true that he asked to be traded to another team. However, the details of his request had been quite distorted. According to him, the Cavs management has omitted the fact they've long been planning and taking necessary steps to trade him. When he found out about this, he decided to just leave.

"I felt they didn't want me there", Irving said in an interview.

Nineteen months later, after his seminal moment of a winning championship, Irving found himself in Boston.

When the previous season ended, Irving was making millions on and off the court. Of course he, together with his team, made it to the Finals. More than that, he had his own off-the-court projects. Yet, he didn't really feel complete.

Irving, sounding quite philosophical, said that sometimes he gets lost in a moment. He tries to mentally list down his goals. He sometimes becomes bombarded with a lot of things – All-Star, MVP, Championship, averages, media perception.

"You start formulating all these false realities and you realize that's not it at all", Irving said.

He added that he always makes a conscious effort to separate himself from all of those false realities. That way, he becomes more attuned with the true reality. Then, he begins looking at the things that he would like to do in his life and decide what would really make him happy.

At the moment, Kyrie may be playing in a different uniform, but the fondness of his former co-Cavaliers is still present. Irving is a man who performs a great balancing act between competitiveness and humility. The 'stay hungry and stay humble' mantra appears to still be strong in his mind.

Chapter 10: Looking to the Future

A lot of people can attest to how easy it is to get along with Irving. Despite all the accolades, he has remained humble. Therefore, it is not surprising that he is now being loved in Boston just as how he was loved in Cleveland.

When asked about the future, Irving has only one thing in mind. He does not want to talk about long-term plans nor contract extensions. He only wants to focus on a 2019 Championship.

"You try to focus on the present – who we have now and what we can do now. I focus on what's important and what we need going into next year", he said in a recent interview.

He just recently suffered a knee injury which resulted in missed games in the regular season. However, Irving insists that he is now feeling good. He is all set for redemption when the new season arrives.

Remember the Uncle Dew campaign where he successfully convinced everyone that he had some acting ability? It has been made into a film and is coming to theaters soon. The sports comedy film, which is entitled Uncle Drew, will be released on June 29, 2018. Kyrie Irving plays the title role, Uncle Drew.

The shoe and apparel company, Nike, just also released a special collection for the star athlete. Kyrie's own Nike collection includes hoodies, T-shirts, caps, sweatpants, and graphic-covered tanks and shorts. This is also part of celebrating the upcoming release of the Uncle Drew film.

Off the court, Irving remains a good father to his child, Azurie Elizabeth, who he had with beauty queen, Andrea Wilson. He got his daughter's name from his own mother, Elizabeth Irving. While his older sister, Asia, is making waves in the fashion industry both as a model and a designer.

Irving doesn't want an easy career, or easy life. Easy is not his thing. He thrives on challenges. With his superstar talents, accolades, and grounded attitude, Irving is set to conquer much more in his career.

"Sometimes you take things for granted especially in your career. But I realized that you must not take people for granted; instead, take advantage of the moments you spend with people you love. You can learn a lot from them. Then, apply those lessons to your life as you go forward. That's where fulfillment comes in", Irving says.

Conclusion

Thanks again for choosing this book!

I hope you enjoyed learning about Kyrie Irving and his incredibly inspiring life and career!

If you enjoyed this book, please take the time to leave me a review on Amazon. I appreciate your honest feedback, and it really helps me to continue producing high quality books.